GROWING THE POST-PANDEMIC CHURCH

A Leadership.church Guide

Bob Whitesel DMin PhD

ChurchLeadership.press

ChurchLeadership.press

The characters and events portrayed in this book are fictitious. Any similarity to real persons, living or dead, is coincidental and not intended by the author.

ISBN-13: 9798671932317
ISBN-10: 1477123456

Cover art is derived from the work of C.J. Martin.
C.J. is a multimedia artist
with an MFA from Herron School of Art and Design,
his work can be seen at
www.cjmrtn.com.

Cover design by: Art Painter

Library of Congress Control Number: 2018675309

Printed in the United States of America

to Rebecca

CONTENTS

WELCOME

For over 30 years I have been coaching leaders on church health and growth. And that includes how to grow after a catastrophe such as a quarantine, a pandemic or other disaster. To help churches navigate turbulent times I earned two doctorates from the highly respected Fuller Theological Seminary, authored award-winning books and hundreds of articles, received both Donald McGavran Awards for leadership and scholarship, while coaching church leaders from many denominations.

Leadership.church is where to find these resources. There you can check out ChurchLeadership.university to find short, helpful online courses to introduce your leaders to the basics of church health and growth. And you will discover information about the MissionalCoaches.network. This is a network of dozens of church leaders who have shadowed me to learn my coaching and consulting insights from 30+ years. There you will also find ChurchLeadership.press with award-winning books I've written to empower church leaders to innovate and change the world.

Bio: A leading voice in the church leadership, growth and health field, Bob Whitesel (M.Div., D.Min., Ph.D., Fuller Theological Seminary) is a prolific, award-winning writer and scholar. He is a founding professor, speaker, consultant and coach with 30+ years' experience. During this time he earned two doctorates at Fuller Theological Seminary in church growth and church change. A national magazine called him "the leading spokesperson on change in the church today."

CHAPTER 1: TWELVE RADICAL CHANGES COMING TO THE CHURCH

How Not To Be A Leftover Church.

Just like "leftovers," something once attractive and desirable but now past its perceived prime, the Church's relevance and connection with culture has been waning in most of the developing world. Social quarantines are likely accelerating this, as small or financially weaker churches are unable to guarantee the cleanliness and hygiene that the public is increasingly coming to expect in public spaces.

Yet historically when calamity struck the Church, it adjusted its methodology while retaining its message. Whether the early persecutions of Nero or the situation in parts of the world today, the Good News has never ceased traveling only doing so in different ways. Today, the Church must again be led by Spirit-guided women and men who are not afraid to adjust methodology while retaining orthodoxy.

The New Rules Of Churchgoing.

A new world has emerged with different expectations in social engagement, cleanliness and protecting our vulnerable populations. This new culture of clean creates challenges for churches with limited personpower and finances. However, Jesus prefaced his Great Commission with a reminder of his power to accomplish it, saying, "All authority in heaven and on earth has been given to me. Therefore, go and make disciples of all nations, baptizing them in the name of the Father and of the Son and of the Holy Spirit, and teaching them to obey everything I have commanded you. And surely I am with you always, to the very end of the age." (Matthew 28:18, NIV).

With such authority and power undergirding our efforts, Christian leaders should not be dismayed by the task. So, how are these new concerns and questions to be managed by people who have faith in a loving, healing God? Here are some rules to follow.

1. Hugging will decline. However, the genuine eye-to-eye smile may replace the hug.

When you haven't seen your spiritual family face-to-face for some time, your first inclination is to hug them. But there will be hesitancy in them and you. And there should be, as scientists attempt to figure out viral spread, origins and reappearances. The pastoral handshake of congregants as they leave will also be curtailed or disappear. But, these displays of affection and friendship may evolve as they have already. The New Testament "holy kiss," mentioned four times in Scripture (Rom. 16:16; 1 Cor. 16:20; 2 Cor. 13:12; and 1 Thess. 5:26) expresses love, sincere affection and friendship. Over the years the hug replaced the kiss, which was further replaced in many congregations by the handshake (though itself was an ancient Greek manner of greeting). The next expression may be eye-to-eye contact and a heartfelt smile accompanied by a slight nod to acknowledge love and respect.

2. Sharing the communion cup will still be meaningful, but in increasingly metaphorical ways.

Some theologies hold that the cup is incapable of transmitting disease (e.g. the Greek Orthodox Church). And, an abundance of caution will cause such churches to undertake new measures. In other churches the power of communion is primarily in the story, its effect and the journey we all share in it. In these congregations the literal drinking from the same cup can be communicated in a myriad of metaphorical ways. These new ways of communicating Christ's efficacious death can infuse new life and relevance for participants.

3. Children's ministry will be disinfected and cleaned regularly, or people won't bring their kids.

Pandemics have heightened parents' concern for what they've known all along: their children spread germs too easily. The reaction will be heightened expectations in preschools, daycares and children's ministries. We have long known in church growth research that young families place a high value upon a church's preparation to receive them. And now cleanliness will add to that expectation. Budgets and staff will need to be adjusted to this increasingly important expenditure.

4. Junior high, high school and college groups will continue to be a hybrid and a challenge.

Young people, who naturally feel invincible, will desire the physical energy created by large gatherings. Youth leaders must embrace new ways for students to deeply communicate with one another, while meeting physically in large groups less often. Social media will take up some of the slack, but face-to-face interaction will remain important for a highly relational youth culture. Balancing safety and relationship building will become the norm.

5. The offering plate will mostly disappear.

People will become accustomed to giving online or giving in a receptacle in the auditorium as they leave. This will remove some of what sociologists call "guilt giving," a natural occurrence when a plate or bag is passed across the lap of a congregant. Instead, online and receptacle giving will allow givers to more thoughtfully consider their giving habits, as Paul admonished, "Each of you should give what you have decided in your heart to give, not reluctantly or under compulsion, for God loves a cheerful giver. And God is able to bless you abundantly, so that in all things at all times, having all that you need, you will abound in every good work." (2 Cor. 9:7-8, NIV).

6. Leaders, greeters, ushers, teachers and other church workers will use hand sanitizer more often.

A nationally known speaker and friend of mine has used sanitizer quietly for years. Some of us kidded him for being so cautious. But at the same time, we knew he was right, he was getting ill less frequently. We just didn't want to overreact. In hindsight, he wasn't overreacting but taking care of his and others' health.

7. Worship will move from

entertainment to experience.

At the beginning of the 20th century the Pentecostal/Charismatic movement ushered in emotional new ways of singing that eventually influenced other emotional genres such as rock 'n' roll. But for Pentecostals/Charismatics the essence of the experience was not the power of the music, but the power of the Holy Spirit moving through the gathered people. Toward the end of the 20th century church music began to emphasize professionalism and showmanship, often resulting in an attraction-oriented expression. Decline in church attendance in the latter half of the 20th century can partially be tied to this move from experience to entertainment. Today we have the opportunity to rethink worship and whether it should be a communal singalong led by a skilled professional or something more internal. Worship will begin to move away from performance to impact. And churches in which people will stay will be those churches where the worship leads attendees into an experience.

8. Singing will be suspect (and different), but meaningful.

Singing has gained ire from scientists who see in its intensity a troubling spread of germs. Yet singing one's praise to God is an integral part of Christian culture and a biblical admonition, "Let the message of Christ dwell among you richly as you teach and admonish one another with all wisdom through psalms, hymns, and songs from the Spirit, singing to God with gratitude in your hearts." (Col. 3:16, NIV). But, where Christians are persecuted, silent singing has arisen as an introspective way to praise. Similar innovative worship expressions will be mitigated by silence singing, electronic media, etc. and can further internalize the worship encounter.

9. There will be different levels of social distancing for vulnerable populations.

People with pre-existing conditions will be ministered to with slightly different protocols. Masks may be continued to be worn by teachers and members of certain Sunday school classes, because their members are susceptible to illness. Specific worship expressions may emerge that minister to vulnerable populations (and in the styles they prefer). Whereas now many worship services are divided by musical style, in the future worship may also be divided by respect and thoughtfulness for those with health concerns. Paul reminded the church at Philippi to "in humility value others above yourselves, not looking to your own interests but each of you to the interests of the others." (Phil. 2:3, NIV).

10. Outdoors will tend to be better than indoors.

Robert Schuller held services at a drive-in movie theatre, because no other rental location was available. But he found that physically challenged people preferred it, because they could participate more fully without leaving the support systems in their cars. In the future, outdoor gatherings will be more popular because they not only allow a natural degree of distancing, but also encourage inclusion of vulnerable populations.

11. A shorter period of time will be better than a longer one.

Because infection spreads not only through proximity, but also through longevity of exposure, people will increasingly prefer experiences that are not overly drawn out. Worship services can be meaningful while not being monotonous or protracted. This is not to say we should quench the Holy Spirit's moving. But we should discern when our human desires cloud us to how the Holy Spirit is moving. Jesus tied worshipping in the spirit with doing so in a true or authentic expression when He said, "Yet a time is coming and has now come when the true worshipers will worship the Father in the Spirit and in truth, for they are the kind of worshipers the Father seeks. God is spirit, and his worshipers must worship in the Spirit and in truth." (John 4:23-24, NIV). That last word, "truth" (Gk. *aletheia*) means something authentic, rather than manufactured.

12. Smaller groups will be more desirable than large groups.

Because viruses travel faster and wider in larger groups, an increasing sensitivity to cleanliness will result in more people preferring smaller groups. Smaller groups already serve as the "connection or sticky factor," connecting people through a smaller intimate group to a larger body. A resurgence in small group attendance and desire should be expected. Also, we will see a greater interest in house churches, those churches of under 50 people. Pollster George Barna predicts that 30-35 percent of all Christians will be worshipping in house churches by 2025. Yet this prediction was made before the recent pandemic.

Now May Be A Once-In-A-Lifetime Chance To Rethink How We Do Church!

Life will go on; the church will grow, and the Good News will be proclaimed. Jesus' Great Commission (Matthew 28:18-20) reminds us the Church is not our responsibility to grow ... but rather our responsibility to participate within. But how will that participation look? The above new rules for churchgoing can give us a glimpse and a chance to adjust our strategies in advance.

CHAPTER 2: WHICH CHURCHES WILL SURVIVE & WHICH MAY FAIL AFTER A PANDEMIC

(and what can be done)

At times when banning gatherings is commonplace,

the faith community will be forced into morphing into something new (or maybe something old, read on). During such times some churches will thrive, but others may struggle. Having coached churches for 30 years, trained hundreds of church leaders and earned two doctorates in the field, here is my forecast with survival options for those churches at risk.

Churches That Will Suffer The Most:

1. Churches with aging buildings and no savings.

During the 20th century having an impressive building was a way to make a church's presence known. Many churches borrowed their way into debt to restore, renovate and expand older facilities. When downturns in attendance occur (and they always do) such churches may not have the flexibility made available by sizable savings. They are vulnerable because they do not have contingency plans for an attendance downturn. If a roof needs repair, a boiler replaced, etc. a church may find itself no longer habitable after a pandemic.

The problem:

Impressive facades, of course, weren't the way the church became known in the New Testament. Paul reminded churches that they should not be known for their physical attire, but instead he encouraged them to "clothe yourselves with compassion, kindness, humility, gentleness and patience." (Colossians 3:12, NIV).

Survival options:

Look for ways to cut overhead by selling, leasing or giving away facilities that drain budgets. Research the correct amount of savings a church like yours should have and create a savings plan. Also, begin to build your church's reputation upon compassion, kindness, humility, gentleness and patience. These are the best avenues to make a church visible in a community.

2. Churches that have overbuilt.

A church building craze exploded in the 1970s and '80s and led to many sanctuaries that are outsized for their current congregation. Even a megachurch (a church of over 1000 attendees) may still have hundreds, if not thousands of attendees. But the cost of oversized facilities and their upkeep may mean that that even these churches have inadequate resources for unexpected expenses or low offerings.

The problem:

This problem arose in part because of a popular 20th century adage (not supported by research) that "If you build it, they will come." And so, the size of the expansion was customarily based on the total size of a congregation's combined services at the time of building. For example, a church in the 1990s may have been running 400 people in an early service and 600 people in a second service with a facility that seated 800. An architect might suggest combining the two services (not a good idea, because it decreases options in times and styles) and combine into one service in a new 1,600 seat sanctuary. "After all," the church leaders reasoned, "400 plus 600 equals 1,000. And, a new sanctuary of 1,600 would give us room to grow." But, when the service times and styles were merged in a large cavernous sanctuary, the church began to run only 700 people. A lack of options in times and styles started the church on a downward trajectory.

Survival options:

Look at ways to right-size sanctuaries. Converting part of the sanctuary into classrooms, welcome centers and prayer spaces can create intimacy in the once larger sanctuary space. Also look for ways to monetize facilities. My co-author Mark DeYmaz in his book, *The Coming Revolution in Church Economics: Why Tithes & Offerings Are No Longer Enough and What You Can Do About It,* outlines dozens of ways churches can lease out portions of their facilities, create local business hubs, develop shared working spaces, etc. to increase income from aging buildings.

3. Multisite churches that own their satellite campuses.

A trend in the 20th century has been for growing churches to purchase older church buildings, theaters and community spaces in which to hold satellite worship services.

The problem:

Many times, denominations did this to encourage growing churches to take on the expenses of a closed church. But, because of the reasons cited above (e.g. the cost of maintaining the facilities) when combined with attendance drops, liabilities were rapidly created.

Survival options:

Lease or rent sites for offsite services, and look for opportunities to sell, lease or give away facilities you own. This promotes long-term flexibility when demographics, styles and finances change.

4. Churches that rely on the onsite Sunday morning offering.

With the proliferation of online giving tools, most churches have embraced online giving. However, some have not, and this creates hurdles for supporters.

The problem:

Even churches that have misgivings about online tithing, offerings and pledges will rethink their strategy when the church is dispersed.

Survival options:

Create and promote an online giving option. Many denominations have a preferred online giving tool you can use. Then educate your congregation about why disciplined giving and online avenues can help a church to thrive.

5. Churches that put on a Sunday spectacle.

Some churches spend an inordinate amount of time and money on the lighting, sound, musicians, broadcasting and staff associated with putting on an elaborate Sunday morning experience.

The problem:

After a pandemic, these Sunday morning expenditures will now be seen as optional as churches are forced to focus more on smaller groups as a way for people to be connected and discipled. And, congregants may discover that smaller groups, which are flexible and meet in neighborhoods, are more enjoyable and convenient.

Survival options:

Many of today's young pastors have created youthful churches that are moving away from Sunday performance and toward more organic expressions of church. I provide a look at 12 categories of organic churches in my book, *Inside the Organic Church: Learning from 12 Emerging Congregations*. Most of these emerging congregations prefer less staging, softer music, audience participation and smaller auditoriums (with capacity around 200 or less).

Churches That Will Survive:

1. House churches, pub churches, café churches and online churches.

These entrepreneurial smaller churches are often dismissed by leaders of more established congregations. But I've been writing about their growth since 2004 (see again, *Inside the Organic Church: Learning from 12 Emerging Congregations*). Typically, they meet in rented or free facilities. Their low overhead allows them as small churches to more easily survive fiscal cycles brought on by unexpected attendance downturns.

2. Churches that have spent their money on staff, rather than spent their money on facilities.

The trend in the 20th century was to expand facilities and stretch staff. This created overworked leaders. Then, when emergencies arose, small staffs were not able to handle the extra workload. But if a church spends its money creating a team of experienced and talented staff, these entrepreneurs can create innovative online options.

3. Churches with bi- or co- vocational leaders.

My colleague, Dr. Jay Moon, describes bi-vocational pastors as those who work two jobs until the church can support them. And he describes co-vocational pastors as those who work two jobs, never expecting the church to support them full time. In other words, the latter have a clear calling to leadership in the marketplace and to leadership in the church. Because the co-vocational pastor does not envision a time where she or he will be in full-time employment of the church, they may be able to make long term decisions without personal financial needs clouding their judgment.

Still, both can be an advantage during times when churches are unable to physically meet. A bi- or co-vocational pastor will become less of a drain on the church finances. And a pastor who is involved in marketplace leadership will better keep her or his pulse on needs in the community.

4. Churches that are young, having been recently planted by a mother church.

Planting a church is an arduous endeavor which requires creativity and entrepreneurship. It takes tenacity, good theology and a balance between ministry and family. The very balance needed in a good church planter can help him or her maintain equilibrium during attendance swings brought on by viral quarantines. And, did I mention that many church planters are bi- or co-vocational? That's another strength.

Good News - Most Churches Will Survive.

Thirty years coaching leaders has led me to believe that God empowers his people to survive and thrive in difficult times. The Bible is overflowing with people who God empowered to overcome adversity. Church history further attests to this. Christians have a grit whereby they come together and work for the long-term existence of the community of faith. It may mean that the facilities, staffing and priorities may change during and after a quarantine, but the Holy Spirit and God's will for his church will not change.

A Scripture reminder is Paul's admonishment, "We pray that you'll live well for the Master, making him proud of you as you work hard in his orchard. As you learn more and more how God works, you will learn how to do your work. We pray that you'll have the strength to stick it out over the long haul—not the grim strength of gritting your teeth but the glory-strength God gives. It is strength that endures the unendurable and spills over into joy, thanking the Father who makes us strong enough to take part in everything bright and beautiful that he has for us." (Colossians 1:10-14, MSG).

What Every Church Can Do To Increase Survivability.

I'll expand upon these ideas in the chapter titled: "4 things leaders should do immediately when something prevents your church from meeting regularly."

1. Focus on making learners.

Jesus commissioned us in *Matthew 28:18-20* to "make

disciples," which in the Greek is one word which more accurately means, "make learners" (more on this later in the book). Therefore, your goal should be to help congregants "learn" during this time, not necessarily congregate.

2. Focus on small groups as the primary venue where fellowship and spiritual growth take place.

Research indicates that most people stick with a church when they are involved in a small group that meets regularly for Bible study, prayer and service. The Methodist movement was founded upon and grew because of such smaller groups. And Jesus exemplified this when he chose 12 learners who he apprenticed to become his 12 apostles. In a small group environment Jesus answered his disciples' questions about theology, history and the future (Matthew 24:1-3), he modeled for them healing and how to pray for those in need (Matthew 10:5-10) and he rebuked the disciples' willful attitudes and ideas (Luke 16:13).

3. & 4. Focus on prayer and serving the needs of others.

During a difficult time, Christ does not want us to make foolish decisions about our health. But he *does* want us to think of others as more important than ourselves. This means considering ways we can help others during this period and thereby let Christ's light shine through us. Philippians 2:1-4 sums this up fittingly:

"If you've gotten anything at all out of following Christ, if his love has made any difference in your life, if being in a community of the Spirit means anything to you, if you have a heart, if you care— then do me a favor: Agree with each other, love each other, be deep-spirited friends. Don't push your way to the front; don't sweet-talk your way to the top. Put yourself aside, and help others get ahead. Don't be obsessed with getting your own advantage. Forget yourselves long enough to lend a helping hand." (MSG).

CHAPTER 3: WHEN CATASTROPHE PREVENTS A CHURCH FROM MEETING

4 Things Leaders Should Do Immediately

During the 2020 pandemic, some states banned all

gatherings over 100 attendees, including church worship services, because of the possible transmission of the coronavirus. Churches with attendance over 100 make up a sizable portion of North American Christendom. And though the average church today has 75 attendees, it is midsize churches that can suffer disproportionately. Without their regular gatherings, midsize churches can nosedive through loss of community and lack of funding. Here are four things every church should immediately consider and especially those over 100 in attendance.

1. Stream Your Services Online, Making It A Part Of Your Church Personality.

Streaming is becoming more popular, but too often it is treated like an afterthought. A pandemic means this cannot be the case anymore. Streaming can be easily accomplished via Facebook streaming, YouTube Live or streaming services such as SermonCast. And you can post them as videos to video hosting sites such as Vimeo or YouTube.

But, don't limit the streaming to just the sermon. It is also important to allow those watching to enter into worship. It is called a "worship service" for a reason. That is because the Hebrew word "worship" literally means drawing people into a "close, face-to-face encounter with God." Therefore, when streaming becomes an alternate to church services, it must not just carry the message (sermon) but also seek to foster a worship experience in which people can feel God is present and moving. Therefore, include prayer in your online services too. Your primary focus should not be to encourage people to stay home (though illness or legality may dictate they do), but to encourage people who stay home to experience God's presence.

2. Expand Funding Options.

Oversized churches may have oversized budgets. And thus, when services are not convened a lack of income can impact a church significantly. Online giving tools have been a helpful option. In the nonprofit sector online giving has increased 15-20% each year. It seems logical that giving may increase when people can do it easily through texting or giving online.

Because many new tools have emerged for online giving, be sure to compare the cost (they vary widely). Also check with your denomination, since many offer an official tool for online giving. An online giving portal allows people to continue to support the church even though their presence isn't possible.

Also explain to congregants regarding how many of the church's expenses continue. Salaries, some facility costs and benevolence spending are just a few of the expenses that will continue. Helping the congregation understand the nature and size of ongoing expenses will remind them why consistent giving is needed to support a faith community in its efforts to do good.

3. Increase Congregant Involvement By Offering More Online Options For Small Groups.

Though smaller groups of 10-25 may still be permitted to meet, wise church leaders will emphasize that Sunday school classes, small groups, prayer groups, etc., can have online alternatives. This will address any hesitancy attendees may have about catching a viral infection. And online small groups allow people who self-quarantine to still receive support during this time. Just like streaming and giving, be sure to compare the many online tools that make online small groups productive and meaningful.

Many people may still resist online groups because they feel face-to-face fellowship is more effective. I once was one of those people. But, having taught classes both onsite and online for 24 years for a large university, I've found that online small groups can sometimes be as deep and robust as face-to-face groups. There are many reasons for this, including not judging by appearance, allowing reticent people to speak up, choosing one's words carefully rather than blurting them out, etc. Regardless of the reason, online fellowship reminds a congregation that a church is a community that communicates two ways, and not just an audience that receives.

4. Use It As A Teaching Opportunity About The Great Commission.

Jesus commissioned us in Matthew 28:16-20 to "go and make disciples," which we touched upon in the previous chapter. But the term "make disciples" can be misleading today. When people hear "disciples" they immediately think of a title, like "the 12 disciples." But in the original Greek, the words "make disciples" was a verb that meant "to make active, ongoing learners." Donald McGavran said, "It means enroll in my (Jesus') school…" Furthermore, Fuller Seminary professor Eddie Gibbs stated, "(it) is an apprenticeship rather than an academic way of learning. It is learning by doing."

If nurturing others to become "active, ongoing learners" is the Great Commission's goal, then we must seriously consider online learning environments which are increasingly being confirmed to be excellent learning platforms. By utilizing discussion forums, downloadable resources, online Bible studies and other tools you can develop more robust learning avenues for your church.

Use this as an opportunity to remind congregants that while technology changes, God's Word does not. Recount how in the Protestant Reformation the printing press democratized the reading of the Word amid protests over the feared loss of hand-written Bibles. And today, there are those who prefer an ink-and-paper Bible (I am one of them) to an electronic version. But such changes in technology present opportunities for church leaders to discuss that though methods may change, "our God's Word stands firm and forever" (Isa. 40:8, MSG).

CHAPTER 4: SAINT PAUL'S GUIDE TO LEADING REMOTELY

(when you can't lead face-to-face)

Look At Paul ...

Some degree of social distancing will most likely be part of future church practices. This will require church leaders to develop new skills and embrace new leadership methods. But for many church staffs, volunteers and ministers leading remotely may feel awkward and unnatural. However, leading remotely is a skill found in the New Testament and the early Church. St. Paul himself provides a fascinating example about how to lead remotely through the letters he wrote to congregations he guided. Here are 12 principles drawn from his writings.

Paul's Guide ...

1. Be personable.

Paul greeted leaders personally. This created a human connection to Paul's remote location (and sometimes his imprisonment). Whether at the beginning of his letters (Philippians 1, etc.) or the end (Romans 16:1-16, etc.), Paul recounted his personal connection with his readers. When critique was called for, Paul even prefaced it with personal histories. In Romans 16 he spends several paragraphs thanking God for those who helped him, but then warns about those who divide the flock. In verses 17-18 he instructs, "Keep a sharp eye out for those who take bits and pieces of the teaching that you learned and then use them to make trouble. Give these people a wide berth. They have no intention of living for our Master Christ. They're only in this for what they can get out of it, and aren't above using pious sweet talk to dupe unsuspecting innocents" (MSG). Paul's greetings not only provided personal salutations to exemplary followers, but also examples of ones to avoid.

2. Reputation is based upon God's work in a life.

Distance, whether physical or created by electronic mediums, can undermine credibility. When necessary, Paul defended his credentials. But he based his credibility upon how God has changed (and is changing) him, stating,

> *"Do you think I speak this strongly in order to manipulate crowds? Or curry favor with God? Or get popular applause? If my goal was popularity, I wouldn't bother being Christ's slave... I'm sure that you've heard the story of my earlier life when I lived in the Jewish way. In those days I went all out in persecuting God's church. I was systematically destroying it. I was so enthusiastic about the traditions of my ancestors that I advanced head and shoulders above my peers in my career. Even then God had designs on me. Why, when I was still in my mother's womb he chose and called me out of sheer generosity! Now he has intervened and revealed his Son to me so that I might joyfully tell non-Jews about him." (Gal. 1:10-16).*

Be ready to tactfully (2 Cor. 5:20) but directly (1 Tim. 1:3) point to God's work in your life if your credibility is questioned.

3. Accept change, yet acknowledge

how God is behind the change.

Don't shy away from accepting change, but also acknowledge how God is changing you. Paul embraced his change, recalling in Gal. 2: 7-10 (MSG), "It was soon evident that God had entrusted me with the same message to the non-Jews as Peter had been preaching to the Jews. Recognizing that my calling had been given by God, James, Peter, and John—the pillars of the church —shook hands with me and Barnabas, assigning us to a ministry to the non-Jews, while they continued to be responsible for reaching out to the Jews. The only additional thing they asked was that we remember the poor, and I was already eager to do that."

4. Go deep theologically, but give them something to do with it.

Don't be afraid to give those you lead remotely something on which to theologically chew. But also make sure it's something they can readily apply. Pauline scholar Herman Ridderbos stresses the general character of Paul's preaching was the kingship of Jesus. And, as a result Paul urged his readers to exemplify lifestyles that attested to living in a new realm. And knowing it might be some time before they would hear from him again, Paul literally gave them something to do. He told them to act upon what they heard, saying,

> *"It's the word of faith that welcomes God to go to work and set things right for us. This is the core of our preaching. Say the welcoming word*

to God—'Jesus is my Master'—embracing, body and soul, God's work of doing in us what he did in raising Jesus from the dead. That's it. You're not 'doing' anything; you're simply calling out to God, trusting him to do it for you. That's salvation. With your whole being you embrace God setting things right, and then you say it, right out loud: 'God has set everything right between him and me!'" (Romans 10:9-10, MSG).

5. Use stories, to help others endure the unendurable.

The early church experienced an increasing loss of civil and human rights because of mounting opposition by the Roman regime. To this predicament Paul encouraged his listeners to embrace perseverance, steadfastness and in the more modern term championed by Angela Duckworth, "grit." Paul wrote to the church at Colossae, "As you learn more and more how God works, you will learn how to do your work. We pray that you'll have the strength to stick it out over the long haul—not the grim strength of gritting your teeth but the glory-strength God gives. It is strength that endures the unendurable and spills over into joy, thanking the Father who makes us strong enough to take part in everything bright and beautiful that he has for us" (Col. 1:10-12, MSG). And in Gal. 6:9, Paul famously intones, "So let's not allow ourselves to get fatigued doing good. At the right time we will harvest a good crop if we don't give up, or quit" (MSG). Learning how God works brings strength to endure the seemingly unendurable.

6. When you must correct, do so with a parent's firm but loving touch.

Paul sometimes had to pen a painful response to his critics. In 1 Cor. 4:14-16 he admonished in a fatherly tone,

> *"I'm not writing all this as a neighborhood scold just to make you feel rotten. I'm writing as a father to you, my children. I love you and want you to grow up well, not spoiled. There are a lot of people around who can't wait to tell you what you've done wrong, but there aren't many fathers willing to take the time and effort to help you grow up. It was as Jesus helped me proclaim God's Message to you that I became your father. I'm not, you know, asking you to do anything I'm not already doing myself…" (MSG).*

As we saw earlier, Paul's critiques sometimes begin with positive salutations. But here Paul prefaces his critique by reminding his hearers of the nature of their leadership relationship, not as a boss to a hireling, but as a father to a child.

7. Face-to-face leadership is sometimes still required.

Continuing the 1 Cor. 4 passage above Paul warns, "I know there are some among you who are so full of themselves they never listen to anyone, let alone me. They don't think I'll ever show up in person. But I'll be there sooner than you think, God willing, and then we'll see if they're full of anything but hot air. God's Way is not a matter of mere talk; it's an empowered life" (1 Cor. 4:18-20, MSG). A key to critiquing remotely is to lay out clearly your intentions if remote leadership is ineffective. Face-to-face leadership may still be necessary and should be understood as an option by all parties.

8. Be authentic and humble.

Paul regularly acknowledged his status, as one Christ appeared to lately, but genuinely. In I Cor. 15:8-9 he recalled, "...He (Jesus) finally presented himself alive to me. It was fitting that I bring up the rear. I don't deserve to be included in that inner circle, as you well know, having spent all those early years trying my best to stamp God's church right out of existence" (MSG).

And in Ephesians 3:7-8, he said, "This is my life work: helping people understand and respond to this Message. It came as a sheer gift to me, a real surprise, God handling all the details. When it came to presenting the Message to people who had no background in God's way, I was the least qualified of any of the available Christians. God saw to it that I was equipped, but you can be sure that it had nothing to do with my natural abilities" (MSG)

9. Put others first, as exemplified by Christ.

Paul knew that each leader who read or heard his letters would need to make a myriad of subsequent decisions. To guide decision-making, Paul emphasized that the arrival of Christ's kingdom meant putting others before oneself. Paul summed this up in Phil. 2:1-7,

> *"If you've gotten anything at all out of following Christ, if his love has made any difference in your life, if being in a community of the Spirit means anything to you, if you have a heart, if you care— then do me a favor: Agree with each other, love each other, be deep-spirited friends. Don't push your way to the front; don't sweet-talk your way to the top. Put yourself aside, and help others get ahead. Don't be obsessed with getting your own advantage. Forget yourselves long enough to lend a helping hand. Think of yourselves the way Christ Jesus thought of himself. He had equal status with God but didn't think so much of himself that he had to cling to the advantages of that status no matter what. Not at all. When the time came, he set aside the privileges of deity and took on the status of a slave, became human!" (MSG).*

10. Reconciliation and transformation are pivotal in the community of the King.

Christ's death and resurrection signified the arrival of his kingdom. A new community emerged which Paul calls, the saints, the elect, the beloved, the called. Over and over he would remind his readers they must decide if they will take up God's offer for personal kingdom life, reconciliation and letting the Holy Spirit transform them. And so, Paul's emphasis upon conversion was not just a theoretical concept, but also a noticeable change in people. Paul famously intoned,

> *"So from now on we regard no one from a worldly point of view. Though we once regarded Christ in this way, we do so no longer. Therefore, if anyone is in Christ, the new creation has come: The old has gone, the new is here! All this is from God, who reconciled us to himself through Christ and gave us the ministry of reconciliation: that God was reconciling the world to himself in Christ, not counting people's sins against them. And he has committed to us the message of reconciliation. We are therefore Christ's ambassadors, as though God were making his appeal through us. We implore you on Christ's behalf: Be reconciled to God." (2 Cor. 5:16-20, MSG).*

11. Be thankful and prayerful for those you are entrusted to lead.

Paul believed thankfulness must characterize every step in a Christian's journey, saying: "And cultivate thankfulness... Let every detail in your lives—words, actions, whatever—be done in the name of the Master, Jesus, thanking God the Father every step of the way" (Colossians 3:15-17, MSG). In addition, Paul's mentees were never far from his prayers. In Phil. 1:3-6 (MSG) he recalls that "Every time I think of you, I thank my God. And whenever I mention you in my prayers, it makes me happy. This is because you have taken part with me in spreading the good news from the first day you heard about it. God is the one who began this good work in you, and I am certain that he won't stop before it is complete on the day that Christ Jesus returns."

Regardless of difficulties, pestilence and/or persecution Paul's leadership is a guide to how to lead God's people in difficult, even remote, times.

CHAPTER 5: eREFORMATION, LEADING ELECTRONIC CHURCH GROWTH

10 Things to Start Doing Now

Not since the 16th century has there been a communication upheaval in the church like we have experienced. Back then (c. 1517) the Protestant Reformation was calling Christians to follow the Bible over tradition as the source of spiritual guidance. And though the Reformers' ideas had been around for hundreds of years, it was a new communication tool, the printing press, that fueled the Reformation's influence.

Churches Are Being Pressured Once Again, Often Against Their Will, To Embrace New Communication Tools.

Today the church is undergoing a new formation, which I call the "eReformation." I chose this word because similar to how the Reformation was fueled by the printing press, a current reformation is erupting as Christendom is being forced to communicate, sometimes against their will, via electronic tools.

Some feel electronic communication is less desirable, perhaps even less spiritual than face-to-face discussions. But we often fail to remember that in New Testament times most Christians did not have face-to-face access with Jesus or even the Apostles. The communication of the Good News was carried in apostolic letters and histories that were carefully written down and then transcribed. While fellowship continued in smaller groups and occasional visits from an apostle, most early Christians learned of spiritual truths and orthodoxy through someone reading ink on papyri.

The Protestant Reformation And Today's

Ereformation

Today electronic communication is transforming how the church communicates in a parallel fashion to how the printing press fueled the Protestant Reformation. The printing press allowed people to own a Bible and to fact-check what their pastors told them. Today the printing press' legacy is thousands of printed versions of the Bible translated into a myriad of indigenous languages.

In the next 500 years how will historians look back upon today's electronic shift in communication? Will future historians see a world health crisis that reformed the church's communication strategies? Extreme long-term forecasts are beyond anyone's guess, but in the near future I see churches that start doing these 10 actions as being better communicators.

10 Characteristics Of The Coming eReformation Church

1. Online small groups will become the majority of a church's smaller groups.

The problem:

The convenience of small online groups along with a growing ability for people to communicate better online, will mean that healthy churches will have an increasing percentage of their small group opportunities online.

The solution:

Start preparing today: Begin to aggressively train leaders in online ministry and communication skills.

2. Authentic worship online.

The Hebrew word for "worship" means to come close to God, bowing at his feet (Psalm 99:5). It signifies a closeness that the inexperienced may find hard to encounter through newer electronic mediums.

Most people have experienced worship while listening to a song on their streaming device, the radio or even a vinyl record.

The problem:

Though such electronic mediums have succeeded in fostering worship, our churches have mostly promoted and fine-tuned live worship.

The solution:

Churches must aggressively begin to improve their electronic worship, not just for the homebound or those who do not live nearby, but also for those who prefer to worship in private. Since worship means drawing close to God in what I call a "face-to-foot" encounter, the church must forsake appearance and spectacle while improving encounter, prayer and reflection during online worship events.

3. People will regularly digest their favorite preachers who may not be national names, but people to whom they can relate.

Many smaller churches with fantastic pastors and worship experiences will grow significantly because they can electronically connect with a larger audience. They will connect to far-flung audiences who can relate to their message, style and culture.

The problem:

No longer does attending a church regularly depend upon proximity. Now attendees can choose a church to which they relate. And that church may be across the street or around the globe.

The solution:

Tomorrow's influencers will be pastors who don't stand before a massive crowd, but instead create a relatable environment of candor, comfortableness and connecting with God. They may sit in a small living room while making the listener feel as if you are present with them. The post-pandemic church and society in general will have a new appreciation for the so-called fireside chat which alleviates some of the fear of the big.

4. Largeness will be replaced by relevance.

Instead of having one large gathering that tries to cater to multiple demographics, mega-churches and even micro-churches will increasingly split up into smaller online and onsite venues where the communication style can be tailored to different cultures.

The problem:

Some will bemoan this as a lack of unity, saying, "Unless we worship together, we won't be one." But the New Testament reminds us that Gentiles worshipped differently than Jewish-Christians (and the Council of Jerusalem recognized this). Yet nowhere did the Council of Jerusalem suggest they worship together, but rather that they worshipped in holiness and respect (*Acts 15:24-29*). And the Bible does not insist that we grow to enjoy different worship styles. Rather, Jesus tells us that worship is to be genuine and true to one's spirit, saying, "Your worship must engage your spirit in the pursuit of truth. That's the kind of people the Father is out looking for: those who are simply and honestly *themselves* before him in their worship. God is sheer being itself—Spirit. Those who worship him must do it out of their very being, their spirits, their true selves, in adoration" (John 4:23-24, MSG).

The solution:

Ask yourself, to which cultures is your current ministry relevant? Then ask, what are the emerging cultures around us? Are they the same? If not, you must start preparing now to hand over leadership to leaders of emerging cultures, so they can be "honestly *themselves* before him in their worship."

5. An increasing number of committee/board/ training meetings will be conducted online.

Church boards, committees and trainings are usually not well attended. This may be because of the rise of the two-wage-earner family where the weekly opportunities for such meetings become increasingly scarce.

The problem:

People may avoid these meetings, not because they don't enjoy the fellowship or task at hand, but because they can't find the time to squeeze them in. Utilizing video meetings with screen-sharing software can eliminate timewasters, such as drive-time to and back from meetings.

The solution:

Experiment with video and online training software to improve your online meetings. Don't view online meetings as a stopgap measure during a pandemic. Rather see them as a time-management method for leadership decision-making that will also foster greater participation.

6. Counseling and theological discussions will increasingly take place online.

Just as the medical community has ramped up their online "see a doctor" services, so too churches will be expected to offer counseling and even theological discussion via an online interface.

The problem:

In the past going to the church for counseling or to discuss something with the pastor could be intimidating for a person going through a crisis. Now congregants can consult these professionals privately from home.

The solution:

Offer online counseling and theological discussion via a personal video chat. And, learn how to communicate your knowledge in a video setting. If you are not a skilled or trained counselor, refer those in need to counselors who are professionally trained. This means learning about online counselors with whom you can agree theologically and pragmatically.

7. Large events, concerts and conferences will still occur, but fewer of them will be sponsored by the church.

Because an increasing percentage of fellowship will take place online, face-to-face events will be premium events that the secular world will be able to stage more attractively than a church.

The problem:

Church carnivals, concerts and conferences will be less attractive when compared to social gathering events staged by secular organizations.

The solution:

Christians must increasingly communicate the Good News through their speech and lifestyle, rather than staging an event to which they hope to bring their friends. Evaluate if church events such as bazaars, concerts and conferences are the best way for your friends to hear the Good News. Rather look to your lifestyle, actions and sacrifices to be the light that shines into your neighbors' world. Jesus reminded us, "God is not a secret to be kept. We're going public with this, as public as a city on a hill...Keep open house; be generous with your lives. By opening up to others, you'll prompt people to open up with God, this generous Father in heaven" (Matt. 5:14-16, MSG)

8. Churches will address society's growing fear of the big: *agoraphobia*.

The rapid spread of viruses and a resultant stringent curtailment of certain liberties means that people in the foreseeable future will be more cautious of largeness.

The problem:

This will mean they will seek churches that are smaller communities or at least exhibit a smaller feel through multiple venues, small groups, etc.

The solution:

Congregations can begin to offer smaller venues as alternatives. Some social scientists (Oxford professor Robin Dunbar for example) have found that people feel most comfortable in groups of under 150 (called the Dunbar Number). Smaller churches can rejoice in knowing that their smaller social groupings will be attractive to more people. But they must prepare now to overcome their natural propensity to exclude outsiders. And larger churches can begin to multiply more smaller venues as alternatives. For them it is important not to let the size of their sanctuaries, which are usually too large and overbuilt, to dictate the target size of a worship gathering. If Dunbar is right, larger churches need more venues of 150 or less.

9. Sharing your faith will become more combative.

I wish this prediction were not so. But regrettably there is something about online communication that lends itself to harshness and loss of empathy. I have even seen discussions about one's faith become more combative in the past decade.

The problem:

This may be because in online discussions it's easier for groupthink to kick in and people to take more radical positions which erupt into heated emotions.

The solution:

Learn how to share your faith, not based upon your opinions, but upon the other person's need. Are they going through a health issue? Are they going through a family crisis? Are they struggling economically or in their career? Listen to their needs and then explore with them the Bible's guidance. As Peter reminds us, "Be ready to speak up and tell anyone who asks why you're living the way you are, and always with the utmost courtesy. Keep a clear conscience before God so that when people throw mud at you, none of it will stick" (1 Peter 3:15-16 MSG).

10. The meaning of life, death and the afterlife will increasingly be on people's minds and must be addressed in church teachings.

Eschatology, the study of one's final destiny, will be of increasing interest as the world grows smaller and waves of illnesses travel the globe at increasing speeds.

The problem:

In recent years the church shifted away from *eschatology*, to topics of how to live a better life here and now. And while that may be important, it is eternal questions that will begin to dominate people's interest as catastrophes circle the globe.

The solution:

Start preparing now: churches need to be prepared with orthodoxy and in clarity to address the issues of life, death and the afterlife.

Remember ...

Jesus told us, "Take a lesson from the fig tree. From the moment you notice its buds form, the merest hint of green, you know summer's just around the corner. And so, it is with you. When you see all these things, you know he is at the door. Don't take this lightly" (Mark 13:28-29, MSG).

Christ knew today's catastrophes would happen. He is not surprised (John 16:30, Rev. 2:23). So, as knowledge of a fig tree tells an orchardist about the coming season, so too must Christian leaders discern the season we are in. It is time for church leaders to carefully adapt electronic tools, the way it once did the printing press, to better communicate the Good News.

CHAPTER 6: THE MOST IMPORTANT THING CHURCHES AREN'T DOING

as they prepare to reopen.

Rebound: The Task Of Reopening Churches Is More Important And Complex Than Realized

Every thought leader I know has created tools

and articles with guidelines/suggestions for reopening churches after a lockdown. But none I've read so far deal with the pressing issue brought out by the death of a young jogger in Georgia. Not just the tragic death of a young man harmlessly jogging through a neighborhood, but also the polarization of the responses lay bare a rift in America not even headlines of a pandemic can replace.

The issue that increasingly and macabrely divides American is xenophobia, a fear of the other. And the answer is an important Christ-like response that churches must extoll and expand ministries of reconciliation.

Renew: What Is Your Church Doing To Energize A Reconciliation Ministry?

During a time of social distancing most churches are focused on repairing their finances and restoring their events. But is this really what the church was created for? The New Testament church seemed largely unbothered with either events or finances. Instead, the New Testament church grappled with the issues of how the Good News was transforming their Gentile oppressors. Theirs was the ultimate cultural barrier, to reaching out to those who persecuted them and accepting them as Christ changed their lives.

The Apostle Paul was accused by a mob of waning in his zealous persecution of outsiders (Acts 21). To this he responded by describing how he had been racially intolerant only to have God change him. He recounted to the mob that set upon him,

> *"I am a good Jew, born in Tarsus in the province of Cilicia, but educated here in Jerusalem under the exacting eye of Rabbi Gamaliel, thoroughly instructed in our religious traditions. And I've always been passionately on God's side, just as you are right now. 'I went after anyone connected with this 'Way,' went at them hammer and tongs, ready to kill for God. I rounded up men and women right and left and had them thrown in prison. You can ask the Chief Priest or anyone in the High Council to verify this; they all knew me well. Then I went off to our brothers in Damascus, armed with official documents authorizing me to hunt down the followers of Jesus there, arrest them, and bring them back to Jerusalem for sentencing. (Acts 2:22-25, MSG).*

But then Paul described his change.

> *"As I arrived on the outskirts of Damascus about noon, a blinding light blazed out of the skies and I fell to the ground, dazed. I heard a voice: 'Saul, Saul, why are you out to get me?' Who are you, Master?' I asked. He said, 'I am Jesus the Nazarene, the One you're hunting down...' Then I said, 'What do I do now, Master?' He said, 'Get to your feet and enter Damascus. There you'll be told everything that's*

> *been set out for you to do.' And so, we entered Damascus ... And that's when I met Ananias, a man with a sterling reputation in observing our laws ... 'Look up,' he said. I looked, and found myself looking right into his eyes—I could see again! Then he said, 'The God of our ancestors has handpicked you to be briefed on his plan of action. You've actually seen the Righteous Innocent and heard him speak. You are to be a key witness to everyone you meet of what you've seen and heard. So, what are you waiting for? Get up and get yourself baptized, scrubbed clean of those sins and personally acquainted with God.' Well, it happened just as Ananias said."* (Acts 22:6-17, MSG).

Personal change was a forceful narrative in New Testament circles. In fact, it might be said to be second only to the change that was brought about with Christ's death and resurrection.

7 Things Churches Can Do To Foster Reconciliation.

1. Learn about the outsider.

Encourage people during this time to learn about cultures that are growing around them. Look at data.census.gov to find the cultures that are growing in your community. Find those that are growing the fastest. Then study their histories, religions, traditions and preferences. Building bridges to another culture begins with learning about the other.

2. Learn not to judge by appearance.

Images in the media can create stereotypes, with deadly consequence. An innocent black man jogging through a white neighborhood generates attention from neighbors who suffered a rash of burglaries. A successful Latina CFO is mistaken for a night worker and challenged for being in an office complex at night. A violent racist claims to have met Christ and been changed on his way to imprison people in Damascus. The perils of judging by appearance are well known, but not widely or well taught. Paul considered the importance of not judging by appearance as an essential "ministry" of the church, stating,

> *"One man died for everyone. That puts everyone in the same boat…Because of this decision we don't evaluate people by what they have or how they look. We looked at the Messiah that way once and got it all wrong, as you know. We certainly don't look at him that way anymore. Now we look inside, and what we see is that anyone united with the Messiah gets a fresh start, is created new. The old life is gone; a new life burgeons! Look at it!" (Acts 5:15-17, MSG).*

3. Learn about the ministry of reconciliation.

Encourage Bible studies, sermons, etc. on the process

of reconciliation. Most Christians know the term but not the conditions. As we saw with Paul's story above, the New Testament world was a very divided world between oppressor and the oppressed. While reconciliation begins with knowing the other, it matures when you no longer judge people outwardly, then repent, release and rectify biases. Promote readings, Biblical stories, testimonials and histories from different cultures that exemplify this.

4. Plan regular unity services.

In one of my books (*The Healthy Church: Practical Ways to Strengthen a Church's Heart*) I dedicated an entire chapter to examples of how churches have celebrated "unity in diversity." The goal of an effective unity service is not to give each culture an opportunity to perform. But rather it is to celebrate how people are overcoming prejudices and rectifying differences. It is a time to celebrate how people who formerly felt uncomfortable around one another are learning, forgiving and changing.

5. Revaluate where you spend your money.

Pandemics decreases in giving, burgeoning facility/staff costs and congregants who are finding their spiritual succor elsewhere (and usually online) have robbed our attention to what really challenges the church's relevance. During a time of physical distancing churches have found their weaknesses are in depending too much upon physical buildings and large events. If you are going to change what you fund, the best time to do that is when you don't have too many funds. I've helped churches navigate these waters of change successfully for over 30 years and learned the best time to refocus a budget is when the fat from your budget is being trimmed and discarded.

6. Pray to recognize your own personal preferences and how they've impacted you.

Have you received preferential opportunities in your life because of your culture, ethnicity, family, socio-economic level, education, etc.? Ask God to show you ways to help others who have not had the opportunities afforded to you. Remember Jesus' words, "The next time you put on a dinner, don't just invite your friends and family and rich neighbors, the kind of people who will return the favor. Invite some people who never get invited out, the misfits from the wrong side of the tracks. You'll be—and experience—a blessing. They won't be able to return the favor, but the favor will be returned—oh, how it will be returned!—at the resurrection of God's people." (Luke 14:12-14).

7. Teach about and expect for people to be spiritually transformed.

People being changed by God's Word and the power of his Spirit is a hallmark of Christ's presence in a church. This is another side of the ministry of reconciliation, because God does not hold our sins against us but welcomes us back into fellowship with him. Paul, in continuing the above passage about the ministry of reconciliation says,

> *"The old life is gone; a new life burgeons! Look at it! All this comes from the God who settled the relationship between us and him, and then called us to settle our relationships with each other. God put the world square with himself through the Messiah, giving the world a fresh start by offering forgiveness of sins. God has given us the task of telling everyone what he is doing. We're Christ's representatives. God uses us to persuade men and women to drop their differences and enter into God's work of making things right between them. We're speaking for Christ himself now: Become friends with God; he's already a friend with you." Acts 2:5:19-20 (MSG).*

Now is the time to teach, welcome and expect God to change humans from lifestyles of bias and violence to a Christlike journey of learning, accepting and forgiving those who aren't like us.

CHAPTER 7: STREAMING SUNDAY SERVICES

8 key things to improve

Having watched many online Sunday services, I've curated the most recurring weaknesses with suggested improvements.

1. Be Your Genuine Self

I found that many watchers flip around to various online services, listening to just a few minutes of each, to find one with which they can relate. It is an opportunity for incognito church shopping. So, be yourself. Be a genuine reflection of the styles, personality and liturgy of your church meetings.

Sometimes leaders consider a video service as an opportunity to try new things or create new impressions. Leaders may convey an impression of a larger live audience than usually congregates. Or leaders may experiment with acoustic worship because the leader prefers the "un-plugged style." At other times, I've seen leaders broadcast the service from their living room dressed casually.

Rather, try to give the visitor a true and authentic sense for the styles, atmosphere and culture of your church worship service. That way if they one day visit a face-to-face venue they will not be surprised. For example, if your congregation dresses up for Sunday, then dress up a bit even when broadcasting from your living room. Paul reminded his readers he was the same person in written word and physical presence, saying, "I do not want to seem to be trying to frighten you with my letters. For some say, 'His letters are weighty and forceful, but in person he is unimpressive and his speaking amounts to nothing.' Such people should realize that what we are in our letters when we are absent, we will be in our actions when we are present." (1 Cor. 10:9-11 MSG)

2. Transitions

Work on transitions to create uninterrupted flow between different liturgical elements, worship and preaching. It may be best to pre-record the service so these transitions can be smoothly edited together. Some churches try to approximate live services by streaming live. Yet because most churches have little experience with online worship, this often creates glitches that interrupt the connection between the listener and the Lord. Distraction in worship is not new. Richard Steele, way back in 1673 wrote the book, "Remedy for Wandering Thoughts in the Worship of God," after he found his mind wandering, stating, "My own disease caused me to study the cure." He found a cure in Paul's admonition to eliminate distractions, "All I want is for you to be able to develop a way of life in which you can spend plenty of time together with the Master without a lot of distractions." (1 Cor. 7:35, MSG).

3. Immediacy

If you pre-record the message, do so only a few days before broadcasting it. It's important not to just re-broadcast earlier sermons, but to talk about topics of immediate concern to the listeners. Talking about suffering and fear are important and timely topics. Romans 8:31 reminds us that when we face calamity, "What, then, shall we say in response to these things? If God is for us, who can be against us?" (NIV).

4. Presentation

Some churches will have the pastor behind the pulpit, re-creating their sanctuary atmosphere for the watchers. Others will utilize a studio format. In both circumstances I've noticed two recurring distractions.

First, when the lessons, verses, etc. are put on a screen behind the speaker they are often not legible. However, if a service is recorded a few days earlier, then these can be inserted electronically. This makes words more legible.

Second, stage lighting is often poor. Most leaders know they need at least two front lights, shinning from slightly above and from the left and right. But most leaders do not know that an additional "back light" is necessary to yield a sense of depth and a 3-D feel. Without at least one back light, a speaker will look 2-dimensional and inauthentic, like a cardboard cutout. Back lighting is also needed at face-to-face events, so make sure you add it to your face-to-face venues as well.

5. Connecting Via Follow-Up And Giving

Place a permanent title on your streaming page with your home page URL. And, every church home page should have three things prominently displayed: how to contact us, event times, location. Most churches also list online giving options. Yet, many pastors feel awkward when it comes to the offering. This may be because they are criticized for overemphasizing or underemphasizing it. So, take time during the week to prepare and record what you will say about the offering. Pray over it and use Scripture to help watchers see that generosity is not only a spiritual discipline but also as something dearly needed during trying times. Paul told the young pastor Timothy, "Tell those rich in this world's wealth to quit being so full of themselves and so obsessed with money, which is here today and gone tomorrow. Tell them to go after God, who piles on all the riches we could ever manage—to do good, to be rich in helping others, to be extravagantly generous. If they do that, they'll build a treasury that will last, gaining life that is truly life." (1 Tim. 6:17-19, MSG).

6. Ignore, Don't Criticize Technical Problems

When you are recording live or even pre-recording, glitches will always creep in. When technical difficulties occur, a leader will usually feel compelled to point out the problem and apologize. But to the many hard-working tech people, drawing attention to a glitch through even an apology feels like public criticism. For most churches online worship expressions are a new frontier. And in that frontier, it is experimentation, failures and successes that should be expected as part of the pioneer life. Jesus reminds us to communicate personally before publicly, "If a fellow believer hurts you, go and tell him—work it out between the two of you. If he listens, you've made a friend." (Matt. 18:15, MSG)

7. Lead People To An Encounter With God

Electronic mediums create physical distancing, but not between people and God. Pioneers like Billy Graham and Charles Fuller used radio in its infancy to lead people to an encounter with Christ. Today it's important that church leaders foster a connection between the watcher and God. Leaders should create times during the service when the watcher feels that God is right there with them, speaking to them and ministering them. A preacher should make this the apex of their sermon. And worship leaders should make this the focus of their time planning and prayer. *Hebrews 4:6* reminds us in difficult times we should, "...approach God's throne of grace with confidence, so that we may receive mercy and find grace to help us in our time of need." (NIV).

8. It Is Normal To Be Worried And Scared, But Trust God

Are you worried, frustrated or just uncomfortable with remote leadership? Paul felt the same way, yet he stated, "I was unsure of how to go about this, and felt totally inadequate—I was scared to death, if you want the truth of it—and so nothing I said could have impressed you or anyone else. But the Message came through anyway. God's Spirit and God's power did it, which made it clear that your life of faith is a response to God's power, not to some fancy mental or emotional footwork by me or anyone else. (1 Cor. 2:4-5, MSG).

CHAPTER 8: THE FUTURE CHURCH

4 long-term negative church effects of a quarantine and what to do about each

In a previous chapter I described what leaders must do if their church services are canceled. In this chapter I will examine long-term negative effects of a viral quarantine and what church leaders can do about each.

1. People Will Get Out Of The Habit Of Regular Church Attendance.

Though most churches are offering online options, many people consider online services a poor substitute for face-to-face meetings. Yet, this may be because in North America we have for years focused mostly on large "event" gatherings. But this wasn't always the case.

In New Testament times the large gathering was the exception, not the rule. Churches in this period grew by meeting in the more intimate confines of homes. Pastors today often worry that if smaller gatherings are emphasized then orthodox and theology will suffer.

But in New Testament times, from where did orthodoxy come? It came from letters of the apostles that were read, passed around and copied. In that regard, the teaching was not apostle-to-person, but letter-to-person. The letter was the medium and the Word was the message. The listeners then were to take that message and live it out as "living letters." Paul wrote, "You yourselves are our letter, written on our hearts, known and read by everyone. You show that you are a letter from Christ, the result of our ministry, written not with ink but with the Spirit of the living God, not on tablets of stone but on tablets of human hearts." (2 Cor. 3:2-3)

The New Testament practice of communicating though letters on papyri is not too dissimilar to online church services and teachings today. People can gather in small groups and read (or listen) to leaders parse the Scriptures and impart biblical truths. Resisting today's online communication methods might be analogous to rejecting a letter from Paul, Peter or John because the author was not physically present. Church history is filled with examples of the Good News traveling through pen-and-papyrus in a similar fashion to how it travels today through an online medium.

The problem:

But as mentioned above, people today have a long history of enjoying the "event" status of a large church gathering. Still, we forget that in the New Testament period (and in some parts of the world today) the church survives and thrives by being underground in small groupings. It is at these times that the small groupings often derive much of their encouragement, insight and community by dwelling on the Scriptures rather than celebrating a large event.

Keeping in mind these factors, we must "balance" our energies, resources and time between "big events" and "smaller, intimate gatherings." Most churches spend most of their time, money and person-power on large events. But the significance of large events may be dwindling in a post-pandemic world where online avenues of community are beginning to grow.

The solution:

The church of the future will no longer primarily emphasize the attraction of a weekly church "event," but rather balance that with an emphasis on connecting with God (which can happen at a big event, but may also happen in a smaller, intimate environment). Thus, tomorrow's churches must create a balance by offering more and better online worship, teaching and fellowshipping opportunities. This means spending more time planning the liturgy and theology of our online environments. And it means spending more effort, staff and assets in creating supernatural online gatherings.

And, with people traveling so much today and with extended families in far off places, online communities/worship can connect people in our increasingly fluid culture. Rebecca and I have found it enjoyable to watch the online streaming service of our church while traveling. We hear the latest news and feel like we're part of the community, even though on many Sunday mornings I'll be preaching at a church somewhere around the nation.

2. People Will Find Alternative Online Communities, If The Church Doesn't Step Up.

The second negative is that people will increasingly look to online forums such as Facebook groups and chat groups for their community. Many of these smaller group formats may not be spiritual, but secular.

The problem:

This can cause people to find their fellowship in smaller affinity groups, but which do not have a spiritual nurturing component. Facebook even stepped up its advertisements about Facebook groups, most likely to provide community in times physical distancing.

The solution:

God has an even stronger desire to connect with his offspring. Revelation 3:20 says, "Here I am! I stand at the door and knock. If anyone hears my voice and opens the door, I will come in and eat with that person, and they with me." And, he created his offspring with a desire for this spiritual connection, as Jesus said in the Beatitudes, "Blessed are those who hunger and thirst for righteousness, for they will be filled." (Matt. 5:6).

To address God's desire to connect with his people, their desire to connect with him and the increasingly online mediums of communication, the future church will increasingly emphasize its small network of smaller, spiritually oriented groups.

3. Workers Will Increasingly Work Online And From Home.

An aspect of a pandemic is that more workers will move online and work from home. This must be true of the church staff as well.

The problem:

Churches typically cannot pay staff members as much as they would receive in the secular world. And so, the church should compensate by offering benefits.

The solution:

One benefit is remote work, which allows employees to spend more time in family and/or travel environments. This should extend to pastors in their counseling and leadership meetings as well. Counseling and management can be conducted via video conference calls. Church leaders should embrace online opportunities and work flexibly to partner with people who are increasingly discovering the flexibility of working remotely. And, church leaders can make more effective use of their time by utilizing online tools, which may also result in an ability to help more people.

4. People Will Increasingly Fear Outsiders.

Fear of outsiders, sometimes called *xenophobia*, may increase when a virus is spreading through close proximity. People will practice social distancing as a reaction, but this can easily escalate into suspicion of the stranger.

The problem:

One result can be that people will be drawn deeper into factional "safe" groups that reflect their own opinions and outlook on outsiders. This polarization can make it hard for outsiders to find a group into which they can fit. And, it can make outsiders feel suspect.

The solution:

The prescription is to remind people that Christ calls us to reach out to the outsider, even at our own personal peril. The story of the Good Samaritan (*Luke 10:25-37*) is a well-known example, for the Samaritan went against tradition, using his own monies to care for a stranger.

The Bible reminds us over and over, that though the Jews were ostracized, they were to reach out to the stranger. Jesus stated,

> *"You're familiar with the old written law, 'Love your friend,' and its unwritten companion, 'Hate your enemy.' I'm challenging that. I'm telling you to love your enemies. Let them bring out the best in you, not the worst. When someone gives you a hard time, respond with the energies of prayer, for then you are working out of your true selves, your God-created selves. This is what God does. He gives his best —the sun to warm and the rain to nourish— to everyone, regardless: the good and bad, the nice and nasty. If all you do is love the lovable, do you expect a bonus? Anybody can do that. If you simply say hello to those who greet you, do you expect a medal? Any run-of-the-mill sinner does that." (Matthew 5:43-47 MSG)*

CHAPTER 9: AN INTERVIEW WITH BOB WHITESEL

Jason Tucker (host): We're excited to welcome back to the Reclaimed Leader podcast Dr. Bob Whitesel. We are going to talk about what's next for the church moving forward. I am Jason Tucker. Here with Jesse Skiffington. How are you doing Jesse?

Jesse Skiffington (host): I know it's a stressful time for everybody as we're trying to navigate through the convergence of all kinds of stuff right now. So, I'm glad today's episode is with one of our frequent guests and a good friend.

Jason Tucker: We have Dr. Bob Whitesel joining us again on the podcast, which is great, because he's always a wealth of information. We will cover a lot of ground and it's really around one idea: what is next for the church? Or what should we, as pastors, be thinking about as we move forward?

Jesse Skiffington: Yes, I'm glad that Bob's joining us.

Jason Tucker: He is our most often interviewed guest. And, if you haven't heard him on our podcast, then you've probably seen his articles everywhere. He is a prolific and very good writer. And he's a knowledgeable church consultant. He is the church consultant under whom I studied to be a consultant. I've learned so much from him and so we are excited to welcome him back.

Bob Whitesel: Good to be here with you. I think I was the guest for your very first show.

Jason Tucker: You are number one, always number one in our house.

Bob Whitesel: How many episodes is this been?

Jason Tucker: This will be episode 137. Yes, and we're excited to have you because my goodness, none of us could have imagined what was going to happen in 2020. Pastors have been under so much pressure and stress. The last time I saw you was just a couple months ago when I was shadowing you on a consultation in Southern California for a megachurch. It was right before this whole pandemic exploded. It's like the entire world changed since I last saw you. Has consulting changed a lot since then?

Rebound & Renew

Bob Whitesel: Actually, I'm busier than ever.

Jason Tucker: Oh, my goodness.

Bob Whitesel: I think what happens is everybody steps back, and they say two things: the world is changing, and we've got to adapt ministry.

We want to adapt our methodology. We don't want to change our theology. So, pastors often look to me, a practical theologian, as their coach or consultant.

Church leaders are wondering, what is the church going to be like in the future? How are we going to do church? As you know, part of my writing/research is in practical theology – the practice of taking solid biblical theology and applying it. In fact, Jason and I first met because he was one of my doctoral students. Even then I was looking ahead and trying to forecast what a healthy church will be like in 5, 10, even 15 years from now.

And now arises this pandemic, which surprises us. But it doesn't surprise God. I see some things that are going to be very good for the church. Other things are going to hurt. So, I've been writing articles to help church leaders rebound from these changes brought about by this pandemic.

I'm calling it, "rebound and renew." Churches want to rebound. And if they can they also want to renew into something better, something more effective. And that's what led to a book, "Growing the Post-pandemic Church."

Jesse Skiffington: I'm glad you're diving into that, Bob. Because our leadership team is asking this question: how do we emerge healthier as a church from this trying time? Our team would love to hear what you have to say.

The Hybrid-Church

Bob Whitesel: First, let me say we're headed into what I think is an eReformation, an electronic reformation. We had a Reformation in the 1500s, a world-wide religious change that was fueled by the introduction of the printing press. That was a new technology and it put the Gospel into the hands of the average person. It totally revolutionized the world. Churches grew and reached more people when they embraced that new technology. But churches that pushed away the printing press technology, didn't want anything to do with it, they suffered.

The same thing has happened today. I call it an eReformation, an electronic Reformation. The way the printing press changed everything, now the internet electronically has changed how we communicate.

But many churches, and some of my clients and colleagues, said, “We don't want to go online. We want keep doing what we’ve done in the past.”

But the pandemic came along, bringing quarantines and social distancing. And now churches have no choice but to embrace online communication to communicate with their congregants and those they serve.

The result is that the future church is going to be a hybrid church, in which we're involved in electronic pastoring as well as face-to-face pastoring. It will lead to new ways for the church to communicate, the same way the printing press led to the rise of book publishing.

Just think of it. From the 1500s until recently, it was the people who wrote books who influenced people, because of the power of the printing press. I think in our future it will be electronic mediums that will influence people in a similar manner. Therefore, it will be a hybrid of face-to-face communication and electronic communication through which the good news will travel during our lifetimes.

Jason Tucker: That is right. We've been talking a lot about how it seems like the church has just catching up to how we live in the rest of our lives. And, we have a hybrid model in a lot of different parts of life. If I sign my kids up for recreational sports, I do it online. I find out where their practice is online. I make the payment online. I show up to a physical experience, but it's seamless between the two. And it feels like church is kind of catching up to how everybody's living their life anyway.

Biblical Principles Of Leading Remotely

Bob Whitesel: Yes. If the church doesn't catch up in communication, some churches are going to die. I've classified eight types of churches that will survive and eight that won't. And, the ones that won't are the ones that hold on to the old way of sharing the good news.

Now let me make something clear. I don't want anybody to change their theology. I'm a very Orthodox person. I believe we need to hold onto a firm Orthodox theology. But we must change our methodology. We see that in the New Testament. As a practical theologian, I love studying people like the Apostle Paul.

My thoughts on this began when a pastor friend said to me, "You know Bob, the Bible doesn't really talk about how to lead over the internet." He was asking how do you lead when you're leading remotely. And I was thinking, yes, the bible does.

Paul wrote remotely to the churches to which he gave leadership. He advised them how to grow, sometimes from prison or from Jerusalem. And we can look at his letters and advice he gave to those he led from afar. I've always been a big fan of Paul. And I've enjoyed reading Herman Ridderbos' book on Paul, one of the best analyses of Paul.

I found 11 things that Paul does to lead remotely. And I labeled this, "St. Paul's guide to leading remotely."

Jason Tucker: That's great. I think I'm seeing churches and pastors that are like, well, this whole thing's going to pass. So, we only have to do this online thing for a short time. Then we're going to get back to the same old way.

Are you hearing that from people? To me, that seems so unthinkable to even consider that. But I I'm sure there are pastors out there who have that sentiment.

New Venues For The Good News

Bob Whitesel: Of course. People like to keep things the way they are.

You can be a church that offers only face-to-face expressions of church. But it's going to limit your reach. It's going to limit the people to whom you are able to communicate.

Electronic venues open up new ways to share the good news. Several years ago, one of my students in Toronto started a church on Twitch.

I asked her about Twitch. And she told me about the online gaming platform. I don't know a lot about online gaming. Pong was the dominant video game when I grew tired of the lackluster videos and repetitious action. But since then I've watched young people create online cities and communities.

We don't want the good news to be absent there too. I'm not saying every church should have an online worship service on a gaming site. But we do need to use the Internet to communicate with people who are homebound either by choice or who can't get to church. Other times people are traveling, and they still want to experience what's going on at their church.

People want the community without being tied down to physically being in that same space with you. So, the more churches can embrace electronic communication without changing their Orthodoxy, the more they're going to connect and make learners of the Bible. That's what we're called to do in Matthew 28: 18-20, "make learners," which usually is translated "make disciples." But the Greek in which Matthew was written indicates the word "make disciples" more precisely means "make learners," i.e. grow people in their knowledge about God. You don't have to get them saved. You can't anyway, that is God's work (Acts 2:47). Our job is to help them learn about God.

But What If I Don't Have Online Skills?

Jesse Skiffington: Jason and I have talked about how seminary prepared us for some things, but not other things. Leadership and online skills were missing pieces in our studies. Then I found the task of leading a church to be kind of an overwhelming time. So, Jason and I have talked about how we need to reach out to the experts in our congregation or maybe in our community. We see doing online ministry as way for us to reach out to people who know more than we do about social media, streaming services, online chat rooms, etc.

Bob Whitesel: Exactly. Many of us have people in our congregations who have experience in electronic communication. And, one of the great things about this, it's reaching a whole other population, the young people in our congregations. People who have grown up electronically learning, they now have an opportunity to contribute to the church. You can engage them in your church by saying: Hey, help us put together a website. Help us put together an online worship service.

There are great examples of this in recent church history. Jason and I went to Fuller Theological Seminary, which was founded by an evangelist, Charles Fuller.

He famously used the radio to reach out in the 1940s and '50s. That was controversial back then, because the radio was championing rock and roll music. But Charles Fuller used the medium while maintaining his Orthodox theology, to reach out to those who listened to the radio but didn't go to church. In the same manner he started a seminary where there would be an openness to new mediums of communication. Today, Fuller Theological Seminary has created new communication avenues for the good news via film, script-writing, television, etc.

Charles Fuller received much criticism for using the radio, a medium that was considered the devil's medium. And then, Billy Graham followed in his footsteps and used the TV and movies as ways to reach out too.

And these new electronic mediums are democratizing outreach. Churches, even if they're small, rural churches, can begin to reach out electronically. One of my former students is in Alaska, I enjoy listening to him preach and the worship they lead. And, I can listen to him every Sunday. Proximity is no longer a driver of church growth.

A Personal Touch In Remote Leadership

Jason Tucker: Can you give us some more insights you learned from studying the Apostle Paul?

Bob Whitesel: I found that Paul did some things that

people forget about today. As you read the epistles of Paul, you'll notice that he always includes a personal connection. He would always recount personal histories. I believe Paul realized that because he wasn't present, it was easy to not feel his leadership was personable. And that's something we forget today. When you record a video or email a person, add a little something about your relationship with those you are addressing. Be personable. Paul would do that either at the beginning of his letter or at the end. In Romans he ended by talking about his relationship with his readers. In Philippians he would talk about his personal relationship at the beginning. Even though those he led were far away, he would include these personal stories and connections. Therefore, I tell pastors, include personal stories about the people with whom you're connecting.

Jason Tucker: That is good to remember, because the challenge of the online world is that it can feel sort of cold or impersonal. What are ideas you see coming into play during this eReformation? What are things that have bubbled to the surface as you've been looking at what's going on in churches?

Online Worship And Smaller Groups As Experiences, Not Attractions

Bob Whitesel: First of all, online worship is going to be more and more important. The fallout from this pandemic is that a fear of viral infections is not going to go away. It's going to continue and at least it's going to continue in waves. And churches aren't prepared for that if they emphasize mostly the onsite worship opportunities.

And the online (and onsite) worship expressions must not be about a performance. It's an experience. People should feel that God is right there with them. They should feel they are experiencing God's presence. So, don't try to create a performance. Instead, create an experience with God's presence. Worship should feel as close to him as if you were kissing his feet. I call it "face-to-foot encounters." The Hebrew word for worship means to come close and bow at God's feet as if to kiss them. That denotes a closeness we should be seeking to experience during our worship services, whether they are online or onsite.

Another way to help people feel close to God is to record your online worship service in advance. If you pre-record it, you can add a graphics, fix things, make the message clearer and eliminate distractions in worship. By doing it beforehand, people can better connect with it.

Another aspect of the eReformation is the importance of online small groups. When I interview people, they usually say they would like to be in a smaller group within the congregation. But they also tell me the biggest drawback is they don't have time. And I say, you don't have an hour? And they often reply, Hey, it's not an hour. It's three to four hours. Because I've got to find a sitter. I've got to drive there. I've got to chit chat with people. And then finally we get down to the real spiritual essence of a smaller group.

But with online groups you can sit down at your computer, connect with seven or 10 of your friends and share your heart. And it doesn't require a building. It doesn't require refreshments. It is the essence of a smaller group without all of the time wasters.

Another key area is sharing the good news. People want to know what Jesus stands for today. They have friends who are sick, possibly dying. And they want to ask questions about eternity, why bad things happen, etc.

Jason Tucker: A second thought that comes to my head is why. Why aren't all pastors embracing this?

Why Aren't More Leaders Doing This?

Bob Whitesel: Well, most of us pastors don't like criticism. But that is actually part and parcel with the pastoral role and even more so when leading remotely. I see that Paul had this problem too. Look at Paul, he was constantly experiencing the ancient version of trolls. He heads to Damascus and on the way has a personal encounter with Jesus. But Paul says later that the first thing that happened after the experience, was that people tried to kill him. And it gets worse as his ministry becomes more powerful (2 Corinthians 11:16-33).

Trolls have always been around. So that is part and parcel with the task of Christian leadership (2 Timothy 3:12). I tell my seminary students that if you aren't ready for persecution, then you shouldn't be a pastor. Trolls, critics, harsh responses, they shouldn't surprise us (1 Peter 4:12-14).

Moving Beyond The Facility-Focused Church

Jason Tucker: Maybe it's good that we're all pushed to be better. Bob, do you think this may change our staffing and our gathering models, that are so dependent on the building? A lot of us older churches have older buildings that require a lot of work.

Bob Whitesel: Well, the new model of planting churches is not focused on buildings. Café churches, pub churches, online churches, churches that meet in homes, these are the new options and they are growing. Researcher George Barna says that by 2025, 35% of the churches in North America will be house churches. These are churches meeting in homes, with very little overhead.

I've noticed that the younger generation is realizing the Achilles heel of their parents' church was the facilities and the expense of their upkeep. Jason has become part of the Missional Coaches Network by training with me and shadowing me in my consultations for a year.

And, in the consultations in which we've worked this year, most of them were struggling with facilities that were a financial drain, their Achilles heel. So, rising facility costs are forcing us to think about more versatile and more flexible strategies. The younger generations are more flexible in the places they meet.

But many churches have few choices and feel stuck in a building larger than they need. They can't find a buyer for their church and they really don't want to sell it anyway, because it holds decades of spiritual memories. For those churches stuck with a big building, there are innovative new ways to leverage a building so it can make money in other ways. Mark DeYmaz, who co-authored a book with me, wrote a fantastic book about how to create new income streams from an older church facility: "The Coming Revolution in Church Economics: Why Tithes and Offerings Are No Longer Enough, and What You Can Do about It." In it, he shows how aging facilities can be leased out for schools or other venues that the community needs. I believe becoming less dependent on a facility and its upkeep is an important strategy, which the online church options help address.

Staffing is another important issue. I'm seeing healthy churches putting less money into facilities and more money into people who deal with electronic communications in the church. And this is not just the sound or video crew. But these are the people who are in charge of social media communication and people who lead online small groups. Since in the future facilities are waning in importance, and communication is increasing in importance, it is theses electronic evangelists who are becoming more important.

Jesse Skiffington: This is what I'm calling a virtual moment. It has forced us to evaluate everything we are doing, things that we had good intentions about. We've always known about the importance of online. But now we are all forced to jump on board. It's sink or swim, adapt in real time.

Online Communication And The Future Of Making Disciples.

Bob Whitesel: Yes, you are right. This is a good thing. It's forcing the church to assess electronic teaching, which we've been hesitant to do for some time.

I taught for a university that was one of the early adopters of online education. And I didn't really like online teaching. I was hired primarily as a face-to-face professor. But when I saw how students who couldn't physically drive to our campus could connect online with my content, I began to reevaluate what I was doing.

I retired after almost 24 years of teaching, but I've brought my online teaching skills to my coaching and consulting firm. I've added an electronic element for every client. And, it is growing fantastically. When a client hires me as a consultant, I include an online preparatory course, called "Church Growth 101" which is part of ChurchLeadership.university. This is basically the first hour of my face-to-face workshop that I previously gave them when I first came to their church. Now they can watch that preparatory lecture anytime in a video, at their leisure and before I arrive. So, it makes my clinics shorter and less lecture.

I have other courses they get during the consultation, including: Church Leadership 101, Church Change 101, etc. Typically, when I would come to a client church, maybe a hundred people would gather for my clinic weekend and my presentation. At this event I'd spend the first hour talking about what are the four principles of a healthy church growth. But now, I may have 200+ people enrolled in that preparatory course. This includes people who couldn't make the live event. More people are enrolled and learning about the subject matter before the first face-to-face meeting.

A pastor can likewise offer preparatory video teachings before a sermon or for a small group. For example, a Bible study group can watch a video created by the small group director or a teaching pastor beforehand, then gather together and discuss it. It creates more time at small group meetings for discussion and less time covering the basics.

And, people who watch a video can have lifetime access to it. That is what I do with my courses such as

Church Growth 101 and Church Leadership 101. They have lifetime access to the content, and it is accessible on tablets, phones, TVs, computers, etc. It makes training more efficient and more effective. Plus, it makes better use of the live trainings because I don't have to lecture on the basics. They've already learned those basics in the video course. Now at the live meetings I have more time for questions and answers. In addition, we have more time to discuss ideas about customizing the strategies for their church.

Jason Tucker: How about church business meetings?

Bob Whitesel: Yes, I often hear from committee members that it is a drain having to go physically back and forth for meetings. Maybe in days when people lived nearby the church that wasn't such a problem. But with people driving back and forth to a church today, the commute time can make the church business meeting less well attended. I admit, you can lose something not being in the same room all the time. But I think a hybrid model of both online and onsite opportunities can increase convenience and thus increase participation.

Jesse Skiffington: I didn't want to miss asking you Bob, because I know you've done a lot of work with multiracial churches, about the significant racial tension and ethnic tension we are experiencing. How do we as church leaders enter a process of breaking down cultural and especially ethnic barriers?

Jason Tucker: Obviously, we're in a significant cultural moment in our country. And I don't think we can have a conversation about what's next for the church, without thinking about how the church should address racism. It feels like we're at a tipping point. And, I remember when I shadowed you that you had some great advice for your clients.

Multicultural Healing, Forgiving And Making Amends.

Bob Whitesel: Yes. As you may remember, my Ph.D. is from the School of Intercultural Studies at Fuller Theological Seminary. That is the school of the seminary that specifically studies intercultural differences, conflict, unity and what the Bible teaches on it. As a result, I created seven things a church can do. I'll get to those in a minute.

But I wanted to mention how I was taken aback by how two crises happened at the same time in North America. First there was the pandemic. Then on top of that was the call for racial justice and healing. However, I noticed that usually researchers/writers wrote on one topic or the other. But I thought, they are inextricably connected. Leaders are talking about reopening their churches with new safety protocols. But we should also be talking about reopening our churches with new intercultural protocols too.

So, I wrote the article, "The most important thing

churches aren't doing as they prepare to reopen." And what we're not doing is also addressing the racial divide in North America. If we are going to reopen with a changed church, let's change more than the cleanliness. Let's begin to clean our hearts and souls from racial division.

In fact, the Apostle Paul tells us we've been given the ministry of reconciliation (2 Corinthians 5:11-21). He describes this ministry of reconciliation as between God and humans AND between humans and one other. You see, Paul was reaching out to the Gentiles. And they were the persecutors of the Jews. The Jews had a lot of qualms about reaching out to the Gentiles. These were their oppressors. These were their enemies, the occupiers of the Jewish homeland who abused and killed innocent people because of racial hatred. And Paul is reaching out to them and seeing Christ change them! That is the background behind Paul's description of our ministry of reconciliation. He sees the Church as bringing divergent groups together while also bringing we who are estranged from God, back to God.

Look at how Paul describes it in the contemporary language of The Message Bible:

> *"Our firm decision is to work from this focused center: One man died for everyone. That puts everyone in the same boat. He included everyone in his death so that everyone could also be included in his life, a resurrection life, a far better life than people*

> *ever lived on their own. Because of this decision we don't evaluate people by what they have or how they look. We looked at the Messiah that way once and got it all wrong, as you know. We certainly don't look at him that way anymore. Now we look inside, and what we see is that anyone united with the Messiah gets a fresh start, is created new. The old life is gone; a new life burgeons! Look at it! All this comes from the God who settled the relationship between us and him, and then called us to settle our relationships with each other. God put the world square with himself through the Messiah, giving the world a fresh start by offering forgiveness of sins. God has given us the task of telling everyone what he is doing. We're Christ's representatives. God uses us to persuade men and women to drop their differences and enter into God's work of making things right between them. We're speaking for Christ himself now: Become friends with God; he's already a friend with you." 1 Corinthians 5:14-20.*

You can see in Paul's statement that this is a dual reconciliation: spiritual reconciliation and human reconciliation. Notice Paul says, "God who settled the relationship between us and him, and then called us to settle our relationships with each other." Now, some people worry that if we emphasize human-to-human reconciliation, we will forget about spiritual reconciliation (human-to-God). But Paul didn't see it that way. He saw it was all as part of the same transforming process. The Message Bible translates the customary phrase "ministry of reconciliation" as "settled the relationship between us and him, and then called us to settle our relationships with each other."

But, reading Paul's words from the New International Version reminds us that the "ministry of reconciliation" is a part of every church's ministry. Paul says, "Therefore, if anyone is in Christ, the new creation has come: The old has gone, the new is here! All this is from God, who reconciled us to himself through Christ and gave us the ministry of reconciliation: that God was reconciling the world to himself in Christ, not counting people's sins against them. And he has committed to us the message of reconciliation." 2 Corinthians 5:18-19.

So, here are seven things almost any church can do to begin:

1. Learn about the outsider.

Learn about the people who different than you. Learn about their ideas, their stories, their worries, their arts, their expectations and their hopes.

2. Learn not to judge by appearance.

We typically stereotype others. Our minds do it naturally and quickly. We look at them and say, "Oh, they're this type of person, because the way their hair looks or the clothes they wear or the way they talk." Call yourself out when you do this. And ask others to remind you if they hear you doing it. Become accountable to not judge by a flash of intuition, but to learn about others as you become friends.

3. Learn about the ministry of reconciliation.

Study how it unfolded in the Book of Acts at the Council of Jerusalem. Remember, Paul and his friends were Jewish Christians. And, they were reaching out to their oppressors, the Roman Gentiles. Paul was reaching out to the oppressors who had Jews burned on stakes, killed and abused. And now, these oppressors are now getting saved! What do we do about that? The Council of Jerusalem (Acts 15) set some guidelines after discussion and prayer. They cautiously deliberated and sought the Lord for guidance, which can be an example for churches today. Yet, most people don't know this wonderful story from Acts 15.

4. Have regular unity experiences where you learn about one another.

Notice I didn't say just having unity celebrations. You must do more than celebrate it. You must learn about one another's expressions in the arts and expressions in worship.

5. Now here is a really important, but controversial

step: reevaluate where you spend your money.

I have coached many upper middle-class churches and I will point out to them that nearby there are struggling urban churches.

As a consultant, I've been in situations where I'm consulting for a struggling urban church and I'm also consulting for a sizable suburban church in the same city. For example, one urban client needed to fix its roof. I think it needed around $20,000 or they were going to have to close when winter came. The suburban church client was talking to me about how they needed to improve their sound system. And they were going to spend $300,000 for the new sound system.

I said, okay, what if you took a tithe off the top of that $300,000 and gave $30,000 to the other church? Some leaders said, they would be glad to. But, other members of the church said, "Oh, we can't do that. They need to take care of themselves." "No, no, no, no," I responded. "You've been blessed by advantages of suburban attendees that the urban church never had. We should be sharing the blessing."

Therefore, I've encouraged churches to reconsider how they spend their money and to be generous giving it away to struggling congregations. Some people label this reparation. But regardless of the term, I reminded my clients that John says in 1 John 3:17 (The Message Bible):

"This is how we've come to understand and experience love: Christ sacrificed his life for us. This is why we ought to live sacrificially for our fellow believers, and not just be out for ourselves. If you see some brother or sister in need and have the means to do something about it but turn a cold shoulder and do nothing, what happens to God's love? It disappears. And you made it disappear."

6. The next step is to pray to recognize your own personal preferences and learn about it with the help of others.

Pray to recognize how you have benefited from either the way you look, the way you behave/speak or the place you grew up. Then listen to others and ask them to tell you about blind spots in your behaviors, ideas or actions that negatively impact others.

7. Finally, expect for people to be spiritually transformed.

Expect for people to change and that you will change as well. Mediate on what it means for you that God is in the change business. I like the way Paul says it: "The old life is gone; a new life burgeons! Look at it! All this comes from the God who settled the relationship between us and him, and then called us to settle our relationships with each other." 1 Corinthians 5:17-18 (The

Message Bible).

Avoiding Being A Leftover Church

Jason Tucker: Awesome, Bob! I think this is exactly what pastors need to be thinking about. In closing, what do you worry about the most Bob?

Bob Whitesel: I worry that churches that won't embrace the latest communication and reconciliation opportunities. And, as a result they will become marginalized. I tell pastors, it's the future of your profession. And if you don't do it, you will be sidelined. You'll be marginalized and a church can be marginalized as well. As the history of the Reformation has shown us, those that didn't use the printing press to put the Bible into the language of the people, those churches became marginalized. And churches that won't participate in the reconciliation of people to God and people to people, will miss the exciting Christian life that the Book of Acts describes. I'm afraid that churches won't be able to afford to stay open, to pay their pastors, to bring about reconciliation between people and to better participate in the mission Dei.

Yes, there is a risk to sharing the good news in an increasingly electronic and polarized world. Still, I believe it is a risk that Christian leaders need to take, if they are careful to keep their bearings in Christ. Let me leave you with this thought. It is from Paul again; he wrote this in 1 Corinthians 9:19-23:

"Even though I am free of the demands and expectations of everyone, I have voluntarily become a servant to any and all in order to reach a wide range of people: religious, nonreligious, meticulous moralists, loose-living immoralists, the defeated, the demoralized—whoever. I didn't take on their way of life. I kept my bearings in Christ—but I entered their world and tried to experience things from their point of view. I've become just about every sort of servant there is in my attempts to lead those I meet into a God-saved life. I did all this because of the Message. I didn't just want to talk about it; I wanted to be in on it!" (The Message Bible)

BOOKS AUTHORED BY BOB WHITESEL

ENTHUSIAST: Finding a Faith That Fills

by Bob Whitesel
www.Enthusiast.life

"It's the best book I've read in a long time on positivity in the Christian life." – Stan Toler, best-selling author and international speaker.

"This practical and powerful book provides every Christian with spiritual impact" – Kent Hunter, author of 20 books, known as the Church Doctor.

"This book can fuel your church's future." – Tom Cheyney, founder & leader of Renovate: The National Church Revitalization Conference

re:MIX - Transitioning Your Church to Living Color by Bob Whitesel & Mark DeYmaz.

"Wow! This is the practical tool for the church that I have been waiting for. Pentecost didn't occur until the diversity of 'every nation under heaven' was present. This book will become recommended reading for all of my seminary students." – Mike Slaughter, pastor, author, speaker.

re:MIX is full of instructive, immediately useful information in a clear and easy-to-use format and includes sidebar stories from church leaders in a variety of denominations who have transitioned their congregations to living color.

THE HEALTHY CHURCH: Practical Ways to Strengthen a Church's Heart by Bob Whitesel

The exercises provided to help increase spiritual health kept growing on me; now I can't wait to try some of them with our leadership team, small groups and congregation.

This book will provide a step-by-step guide for developing a church according to God's purposes. Besides, it gives you a great list of references to further and deeper study.

In addition to practical, biblical teaching based on the latest research, Whitesel offers is seven exercises to help strengthen your church's heart.

CURE FOR THE COMMON CHURCH: God's Plan to Restore Church Health by Bob Whitesel

"Immensely practical with needed tools to lead any church through a revitalization journey." – Ed Stetzer, Billy Graham Distinguished Chair of Church, Mission, and Evangelism at Wheaton College and Executive Director, Billy Graham Center at Wheaton College.

"Need help diagnosing your church's spiritual illness? THE DOCTOR IS IN!" – Dave Workman, Former Sr. Pastor, Vineyard Church, Cincinnati.

"Step-by-step instructions & a rich array of resources, this book not only helps self-examination but will also bring about church health & growth." – Eddie Gibbs, author & former Donald McGavran Professor of Church Growth, Fuller Seminary.

ORGANIX: Signs of Leadership in a Changing Church by Bob Whitesel

"As usual, Bob Whitesel brings fresh new insights to frustrating old problems for local church leaders. In this refreshing book, readers will find important keys to managing the complexities of both the 'organism' and the 'organization' of the contemporary church." – Charles Arn, author and professor.

"Whitesel gives wise insight and practical principles about millennial leadership. Bob's years of teaching, study and practice come forth very clearly in this book. I was impressed by the book's freshness, clarity, and layout. Great job, Bob!" – Joel Comiskey, Ph.D., author and president of Joel Comiskey Group.

WAYPOINT: Navigating Your Spiritual Journey by Bob Whitesel

A step-by-step guide for sharing your faith with others.

Includes the entertaining story of Oksana, a young traveler who is tired of religion and goes to the Australian Outback looking for God. Follow her winding journey through some of the most significant events of the last 20 years, as she encounters the terror of 9-11, loses her faith, only to find it again in the most remarkable place. In each chapter follow her unfolding story as she searches for a long-lost child, tries to repair a relationship with an abusive first husband, and eventually finds peace and significance in the Punjab providence of India.

SPIRITUAL WAYPOINTS: Helping Others Navigate the Journey by Bob Whitesel

Outreach Magazine Resource of the Year Runner-up

"The idea of 'waypoints' is a creative metaphor certain to stimulate new perspectives." – Warren Bird, vice president for research and equipping at the Evangelical Council for Financial Accountability (ECFA) and former LeadNet Director of Research.

"He shows that individuals bounce back and forth as they face fresh challenges on their spiritual journey. And, he provides ample illustrations of people at various stages in their spiritual journey drawn from his extensive consulting experience." – Eddie Gibbs, author & former Donald McGavran Professor of Church Growth, Fuller Seminary.

Whitesel interviews 16 leading evangelicals, giving voice to their stories of spiritual waypoints including: Tony Campolo, Dan Kimball, Len Sweet, Shane Claiborne, Scot McKnight, Sally Morgenthaler, Larry Osborne and more.

PREPARING FOR CHANGE REACTION: How to Introduce Change in Your Church by Bob Whitesel

Outreach Magazine Co-Resource of the Year

This *Handbook on Church Change* is the result of Bob Whitesel's Ph.D. work at Fuller Seminary on how to bring about positive church change.

Everything you need to know to bring about positive change. Sermon ideas ... and the first complete "biblical theology of change."

"Bob Whitesel is the key spokesman on change theory in the church today." – Dr. Gary McIntosh, Talbot School of Theology

INSIDE THE ORGANIC CHURCH: Learning From 12 Emerging Congregations by Bob Whitesel

Co-Resource of the Year, Outreach Magazine

Outreach Magazine said: "Many postmodern resources assume that every reader understands the nuances and definitions of the postmodern missional movement. This book not only gives a clear definition and background of the movement, but it also provides case studies and practical learning tools from organic communities across the globe."

Go inside congregations that draw upon ancient traditions and modern technologies to create a spiritual community and shows how the practices of the "organic church" can be instructive for all those wishing to reach today's world with the gospel of Christ.

GROWTH BY ACCIDENT, DEATH BY PLANNING: How NOT to Kill a Growing Congregation by Bob Whitesel

A book that continues to be the definitive guide to church growth and health. In the plain, direct style that is his hallmark, the author lays out where churches go wrong in their planning and how they can correct themselves. Eventually and typically, the leaders of the growing church begin to read church growth books, periodicals and case studies.

Often the leaders begin to make planning decisions that are similar to other churches they perceive to be in their situation. The majority of larger churches have adopted plans that have plateaued their congregations, the growing church follows suit.

STAYING POWER: Why People Leave the Church Over Change (AND WHAT YOU CAN DO ABOUT IT) by Bob Whitesel

A guide to working for change in the congregation without losing members. Filled with numerous examples of actual congregations that have either succumbed to conflict over change or worked through it, *Staying Power* will be helpful to all congregational leaders who wish to introduce substantive new directions into the life of the church without alienating a significant portion of its membership.

Bob Whitesel gives incredible insight to why change doesn't work and how to do it better. It is a great resource for anyone who faces the challenge of leading change in an established church.

A HOUSE DIVIDED: Bridging the Generation Gaps in Your Church by Bob

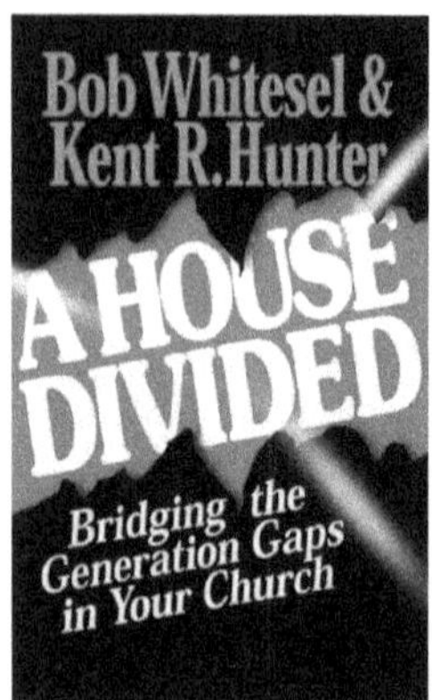

Whitesel and Kent R. Hunter

The first book to awake the church to generational conflicts and how to overcome them … creating a multi-generational church.

Based on 9 years of field research, "A House Divided: Bridging the Generation Gaps in Your Church," gives 7 steps to move any church from a one-generational bias, to a healthy Multi-Generational balance."

One of the most substantial church growth books we have seen in years." – C. Peter Wagner, author of 30+ books & dean of the Church Growth Movement.

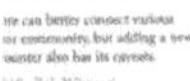
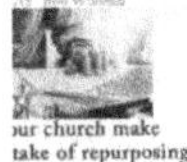
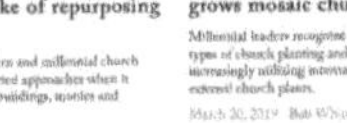

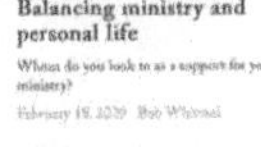

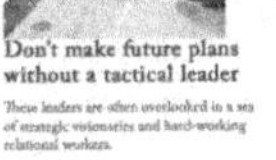

300+ PUBLISHED ARTICLES WRITTEN BY BOB WHITESEL

CLICK > www.biblicalleadership.com/contributors/bobwhitesel/

for a sample of 60+ articles published by Biblical Leadership Magazine.

DISCOVER MORE AT ...

ChurchLeadership.university

Grow Learn Enjoy

Communication
Competent
Reconciliation
7Systems.church
Unified
Supernatural
Involved
Regeneration

8steps4change.church

Leadership.tours

Travel Meet Learn Renew

MISSIONAL COACHES NETWORK
This is to certify that
BENJAMIN ANDREW KING
Bob Whitesel D.Min. Ph.D.
Certified
MISSIONAL
COACH
SOUL KITCHEN

Printed in the USA
CPSIA information can be obtained
at www.ICGtesting.com
LVHW040053170724
785730LV00031B/372

9 798671 932317